What Are the Chances?

by Katie Sharp
illustrated by Jason Chin

 HOUGHTON MIFFLIN   BOSTON

Printed in China

ISBN 10: 0-618-89902-2
ISBN 13: 978-0-618-89902-9

12 13 14 15 0940 16 15 14 13
4500432010

The commotion from Mrs. Baker's fourth-grade classroom caught the principal's attention.

"What's happening in here?" Mr. Clark asked.

"Who would like to tell Mr. Clark about our raffle?" Mrs. Baker asked. A sea of hands burst into the air.

Mrs. Baker pointed to Justin.

"We're having a raffle to raise money for a classroom computer," Justin explained. "Water Wave Park has donated four season passes that we're going to raffle off. We're going to sell raffle tickets tomorrow."

"Wow," said Mr. Clark. "How many raffle tickets will you be selling?"

"We hope to sell one hundred tickets altogether," Mrs. Baker replied.

Just then the bell rang. Justin and Clay gathered their things and walked home together as they always did.

"I love Water Wave Park," said Justin. "It would be so awesome to win those season passes. I mean, how cool would it be to swim in the giant wave pool every day this summer?"

Read·Think·Write Is there a way to predict who will win a raffle?

"That would be great," Clay agreed with Justin. "Hey, because there are four passes, how about we share them if one of us wins? We'll have a better chance of winning if we do."

"That's a great idea!" said Justin. "We'd want to go together all the time anyway."

"Let's go to my house and decide how many tickets we should buy," said Clay. "We can use what Mrs. Baker taught us about probability to figure out our best chances to win."

"Sounds like a plan!" said Justin. "Let's go!"

Read·Think·Write Are Clay and Justin right that they have a better chance of winning if they share the prize?

Justin and Clay sat at the table in Clay's kitchen.

"How many raffle tickets do you think we need to buy in order to win?" Justin asked.

"Well, if we bought all one hundred tickets, we'd win for sure!" Clay laughed. "And if we bought half of the tickets," Justin added, "the probability that we'd win would be half, or 50 percent."

"Those are great odds!" said Clay. "But I can't afford to buy that many raffle tickets."

"Me neither," Justin said. "Plus, Mrs. Baker said that in order to be fair, we can buy only five tickets each."

"But because we want to share the prize," Clay reminded him, "it's like we can buy ten tickets!"

Read·Think·Write Is Clay right when he says if they bought all one hundred tickets they would win for sure? Why?

"First let's figure out the probability of winning if we bought just one ticket," said Clay. "We know there will be just one winner. So we divide one by the number of chances of winning, which is the number of raffle tickets sold."

Clay wrote this on his paper:

probability of winning = 1 winner/number of tickets sold

"How do we know how many tickets will sell?" asked Justin.

"We are talking about four season passes to Water Wave Park," Clay said. "Everyone wants them. I think we can say that all one hundred tickets will sell."

"You're right," said Justin.

Clay changed what he had written to show that one hundred tickets would be sold:

probability of winning = 1 winner/100 tickets sold

"If we buy just one ticket," said Clay, "our chance of winning would be one out of one hundred. That's the same as 1 percent."

Read·Think·Write How did Clay figure out that one out of one hundred is the same as 1 percent?

"One percent? Those chances don't sound so good," said Justin.

"No kidding," said Clay. "Let's see what happens if we each buy one ticket. We have to multiply by two."

probability of winning =
1 winner/100 tickets sold x 2 tickets bought = .02

"Two percent is not much better than one percent," said Justin.

"I think there's only one way to win," said Clay. "We need to buy as many tickets as Mrs. Baker will allow us to."

Clay changed the problem to figure out the probability of winning with a total of ten tickets:

probability of winning =
1 winner/100 tickets sold x 10 tickets bought = .10

"With ten tickets," Clay said, "we have a 10 percent chance of winning."

"That sounds much better," said Justin.

The next day, Clay and Justin each bought five raffle tickets. After all the tickets were sold, Mrs. Baker pulled the winning ticket from the box. "Our winner is . . . Melissa!"

Melissa screamed with excitement.

"How many tickets did you buy, Melissa?" Justin asked.

"Just one," she giggled.

"But Justin and I bought ten tickets altogether," said Clay. "Our chances of winning were better, but we didn't win!"

"You did indeed have the greatest probability of winning the raffle," said Mrs. Baker. "But you didn't win. So what does that tell you about probability?"

Read·Think·Write Clay and Justin bought ten tickets, and Melissa bought one. If one hundred tickets were sold, how many tickets did the other students buy altogether?

1. If Mrs. Baker did not put a limit on the number of tickets a student could buy, what is the probability that a student who bought 6 tickets would win the raffle?

2. Change the number of tickets sold to 150. Now what are the chances that a student who bought 10 tickets would win?

3. Using what you know about probability, add a new ending to the story, in which Clay answers Mrs. Baker's question.

Activity

Predict Outcomes How many students are in your class? How many students are boys? How many are girls? If the teacher calls on a student, what is the chance the student will be a girl? Use number tiles to set up the probability problem.